AMERICA'S
Prayers

GIBBS SMITH, PUBLISHER

First Edition
05 04 03 02 01   5 4 3 2 1

© 2001 Gibbs Smith, Publisher
All rights reserved.

Published by
Gibbs Smith, Publisher
P.O. Box 667
Layton, Utah 84041

Orders: (1-800) 748-5439
www.gibbs-smith.com

Edited by Suzanne Gibbs Taylor
Designed and produced by Axiom Designed Communications
Printed and bound in the U.S.A.

ISBN 1-58685-163-2

God of liberty,
we acknowledge Your reign.
For the freedom of our land
for the rights we possess,
for the security of our laws,
we praise You and thank You.

Give guidance to our leaders,
watch over those
who serve their country,
raise up the poor,
and exalt the humble.

Make our nation great and strong,
renowned in wisdom,
prosperous in virtue,
and renewed in faith.
Destroy all signs of division:
take away hatred and violence;
fill us with Your peace.
Make us one people,
united in praising You,
through Christ our Lord.

ANONYMOUS

We gather together to ask the Lord's blessing;
He chastens, and hastens his will to make known;
The wicked oppressing now cease from distressing.
Sing praises to his name; He forgets not his own.
Beside us to guide us, our God with us joining,
Ordaining, maintaining his kingdom divine;
So from the beginning the fight we were winning;
Thou, Lord, wast at our side; all glory be thine!
We all do extol thee, thou leader triumphant,
And pray that thou still our defender wilt be.
Let thy congregation escape tribulation;
Thy name be ever praised! O Lord, make us free!

ANONYMOUS

I sought the Lord, and he heard me,
and delivered me from all my fears.

PSALM 34:4

*O*ur Father and our God,
We praise You for your goodness to our nation,
Giving us blessings far beyond what we deserve.

Yet we know all is not right with America.
We deeply need a moral and spiritual renewal
To help us meet the many problems we face.

Convict us of sin. Help us to turn to You in
Repentance and faith. Set our feet on the path
Of Your righteousness and peace.
We pray today for our nation's leaders.
Give them the wisdom to know what is right,
And the courage to do it.

You have said, "Blessed is the Nation
whose God is the Lord."
May this be a new era for America,
As we humble ourselves and acknowledge You alone
As our Savior and LORD.

BILLY GRAHAM

O Lord, purge our eyes to see
Within the seed a tree,
Within the glowing egg a bird,
Within the shroud a butterfly.
Till, taught by such we see
Beyond all creatures, Thee.

CHRISTINA ROSSETTI

*P*rotect me, dear Lord;
My boat is so small,
And your sea is so big.

*M*ake us worthy, Lord
to serve our fellow-men
throughout the world
Who live and die in poverty and hunger.
Give them, through our hands,
This day their daily bread;
And by our understanding love,
Give peace and joy.

MOTHER THERESA

Almighty God: Our sons, pride of our nation,
this day have set upon a mighty endeavor, a struggle
to preserve our Republic, our religion, and our
civilization, and to set free a suffering humanity.
Lead them straight and true;
give strength to their arms, stoutness to their hearts,
steadfastness in their faith.
And, O Lord, give us faith. Give us faith in Thee;
faith in our sons; faith in each other;
faith in our united crusade.
Let not the keenness of our spirit ever be dulled.
Let not the impacts of temporary events, of temporal
matters of but fleeting moment—let not these deter
us in our unconquerable purpose.
With Thy blessing, we shall prevail over the unholy
forces of our enemy. Lead us to the saving of our
country, and with our sister nations into a world
unity that will spell a sure peace—a peace
invulnerable to the schemings of unworthy men.
And a peace that will let all of men live in freedom,
reaping the just rewards of their honest toil.
Thy will be done, Almighty God. Amen.

FRANKLIN DELANO ROOSEVELT

FAITH

May all I say and all I think
be in harmony with Thee,
God within me, God beyond me,
Maker of the Trees.

NATIVE AMERICAN (CHINOOK)

$\mathcal{C}$reator, open our hearts
to peace and healing between all people.

Creator, open our hearts
to provide and protect for all children of the earth.

Creator, open our hearts
to respect for the earth, and all the gifts of the earth.

Creator, open our hearts
to end exclusion, violence, and fear among all.

Thank you for the gifts of this day and every day.

NATIVE AMERICAN (MICMAC, ALYCIA LONGRIVER)

$\mathcal{O}$ our Father, the Sky, hear us
and make us strong.
O our Mother, the Earth, hear us
and give us support.
O Spirit of the East,
send us your wisdom.
O Spirit of the South,
may we tread your path.
O Spirit of the West,
may we always be ready for the long journey.
O Spirit of the North, purify us
with your cleansing winds.

NATIVE AMERICAN (SIOUX)

*A*ngel of God,
my guardian dear,
through whom God's love commits Thee here,
ever this day,
be at my side
to light and guard,
to rule and guide.

CATHOLIC PRAYER TO GUARDIAN ANGEL

*H*umbly we pray that this mind
may be steadfast in us,
and that through these our hands,
and the hands of others
to whom thou shalt give the same spirit,
thou wilt vouchsafe to endow
the human family with new mercies.

FRANCIS BACON

*A*lmighty, Everlasting God,
the Protector of all those who put their trust in Thee:
hear our prayers in behalf of Thy servants
who sail their vessels beneath the seas.
We beseech Thee to keep in Thy sustaining care
all who are in submarines, that they may be delivered
from the hidden dangers of the deep.
Grant them courage, and a devotion to fulfill their duties,
that they may better serve Thee and their native land.
Though acquainted with the depths of the ocean,
deliver them from the depths of despair
and the dark hours of the absence of friendliness
and grant them a good ship's spirit.
Bless all their kindred and loved ones
from whom they are separated.
When they surface their ships,
may they praise Thee for Thou art there
as well as in the deep.
Fill them with Thy Spirit
that they may be sure in their reckonings,
unwavering in duty, high in purpose,
and upholding the honor of their nation. Amen.

THE SUBMARINER'S PRAYER

TRUTH

$\mathcal{O}$ God, we pray for all those in our world
who are suffering from injustice:
For those who are discriminated against
because of their race, color or religion;
For those imprisoned
for working for the relief of oppression;
For those who are hounded
for speaking the inconvenient truth;
For those tempted to violence
as a cry against overwhelming hardship;
For those deprived of reasonable health and education;
For those suffering from hunger and famine;
For those too weak to help themselves
and who have no one else to help them;
For the unemployed who cry out
for work but do not find it.
We pray for anyone of our acquaintance
who is personally affected by injustice.
Forgive us, Lord, if we unwittingly share in the conditions
or in a system that perpetuates injustice.
Show us how we can serve your children
and make your love practical by washing their feet.

MOTHER THERESA

$\mathcal{D}$ear Lord,
I may not see the sun and moon lose their light.
I may not witness rivers turn red,
or stars fall from the sky.
Yet there are times when my world
becomes unhinged
and the foundations of what I believe
crack and dissolve.
Give me the grace to believe that
Your power is at work in the turmoil of my life.
Lead me to remember that Your power
is greater than all evil,
and though the world may rock and sometimes break,
it will in time be transformed by Your Love.

AUTHOR UNKNOWN

*L*ord, make me an instrument of Your peace;
where there is hatred, let me sow love;
where there is injury, pardon;
where there is doubt, faith;
where there is despair, hope;
where there is darkness, light;
and where there is sadness, joy.

ST. FRANCIS OF ASSISI

All mighty Father, whose way is in the sea
and whose paths are in the great waters, whose
command is over all and whose love never faileth:
Let me be aware of Thy presence
and obedient to Thy will.
Keep me true to my best self,
guarding me against dishonesty in purpose and in deed,
and helping me so to live
that I can stand unashamed and unafraid before my
shipmates, my loved ones, and Thee.

Protect those in whose love I live.
Give me the will to do the work of a man
and to accept my share of responsibilities
with a strong heart and a cheerful mind.
Make me considerate of those
entrusted to my leadership
and faithful to the duties my country
has intrusted to me.
Let my uniform remind me daily
of the traditions of the Service of which I am a part.

If I am inclined to doubt, steady my faith;
if I am tempted, make me strong to resist;
if I should miss the mark,
give me courage to try again.
Guide me with the light of truth
and keep before me the life of Him
by whose example and help I trust
to obtain the answer to my prayer,
Jesus Christ, our Lord.

WORLD WAR II NAVAL SERVICEMAN

$\mathcal{D}$isturb us, Lord, when
We are too well pleased with ourselves,
When our dreams have come true
Because we have dreamed too little,
When we arrived safely
Because we sailed too close to the shore.

Disturb us, Lord, when
With the abundance of things we possess
We have lost our thirst
For the waters of life;
Having fallen in love with life,
We have ceased to dream of eternity
And in our efforts to build a new earth,
We have allowed our vision
Of the new Heaven to dim.

Disturb us, Lord, to dare more boldly,
To venture on wider seas
Where storms will show your mastery;
Where losing sight of land,
We shall find the stars.

We ask You to push back
The horizons of our hopes;
And to push into the future
In strength, courage, hope, and love.

SIR FRANCIS DRAKE

May peace prevail on earth.

WORLD PEACE PRAYER, MASAHISA GOI

*I*f there is to be peace in the world,
There must be peace in the nations.

If there is to be peace in the nations,
There must be peace in the cities.

If there is to be peace in the cities,
There must be peace between neighbors.

If there is to be peace between neighbors,
There must be peace in the home.

If there is to be peace in the home,
There must be peace in the heart.

LAO-TSE

When I despair,
I remember that all through history
the ways of truth and love have always won.
There have been tyrants, and murderers,
and for a time they can seem invincible,
but in the end they always fall.

Think of it—always.

MAHATMA GANDHI

*M*ay I be filled with loving kindness.
May I be well.
May I be peaceful and at ease.
May I be happy.

ANCIENT TIBETAN BUDDHIST MEDITATION

When I am called to duty, God,
Whenever flames may race,
Give me strength to save some life,
Whatever be its age.
Help me embrace a little child,
Before it is too late,
Or save some older person
From the horror of that fate.
Enable me to be alert
And hear the weakest shout,
And quickly and efficiently put the fire out.
I want to fill my calling,
And give the best in me,
To guard my every neighbor,
And his property.
And if according to our fate,
I have to lose my life,
Please bless with Your protecting hand,
My children and my mate.

A FIREFIGHTER'S PRAYER

*D*ear God, I am proud to be wed to one who defends freedom and peace. My challenges are many and I pray for your love and guidance to meet them. Special to me are the symbols representing my religion, country, community, and home. I pray for the wisdom and grace to be true to their meaning. You are the symbol of my religious beliefs, and the source of my strength. Because my life is full of change, I cherish the solid and constant spiritual foundation that you provide. Help me, Lord, to be an example of your teachings. My national flag represents freedom. Let me never forget, or take for granted, the hope it shows to the world. Bless those who have made sacrifices for freedom. As I enter the gateway to a military community, guide me to reach out to others and keep it a wholesome place. May my charity be given without thought to personal rewards. My wedding ring represents eternity and never-ending love. Let me celebrate all of the joys of our togetherness and find comfort in them during times of separation.

I pray, also, we are spared the ultimate sacrifice of duty to country. My house is a symbol of our family and its unity. It is the place where we share memories of the past and build dreams of the future. Make willing my heart and hands to do even the smallest tasks that will make our house a better home. Thank you, God, for daily being with us as we live in the Army. Please grant us your continued blessings, increased strength, and infinite guidance, as we live to your honor and glory.

AN ARMY SPOUSE

Give us, O Lord, steadfast hearts,
which no unworthy thought can drag downwards;
unconquered hearts,
which no tribulation can wear out,
upright hearts,
which no unworthy purpose may tempt aside.

Bestow upon us also, O Lord our God,
understanding to know Thee,
diligence to seek Thee,
wisdom to find Thee,
and a faithfulness that may finally embrace Thee.

ST. THOMAS AQUINAS

Mother, sing me a song
That will ease my pain,
Mend broken bones,
Bring wholeness again.

Catch my babies
When they are born,
Sing my death song,
Teach me how to mourn.

Show me the medicine
Of the healing herbs,
The value of spirit,
The way I can serve.

Mother, heal my heart
So that I can see
The gifts of yours
That can live through me.

A NATIVE AMERICAN HEALING PRAYER

The Lord is my shepherd; I shall not want.

He maketh me to lie down in green pastures,
he leadeth me beside the still waters.

He restoreth my soul: he leadeth me in the paths of
righteousness for his name's sake.

Yea, though I walk through the valley of the
shadow of death, I will fear no evil: for thou
art with me; thy rod and thy staff they comfort me.

Thou preparest a table before me in the presence of
mine enemies: thou anointest my head with oil;
my cup runneth over.

Surely goodness and mercy shall follow me all the
days of my life: and I will dwell
in the house of the Lord for ever.

PSALM 23

I asked God for strength, that I might achieve,
I was made weak, that I might learn humbly to obey.
I asked for health, that I might do great things,
I was given infirmity, that I might do better things.
I asked for riches, that I might be happy,
I was given poverty, that I might be wise.
I asked for power, that I might have the praise of men,
I was given weakness, that I might feel the need of God.
I asked for all things, that I might enjoy life,
I was given life, that I might enjoy all things.
I got nothing that I asked for—but everything
I had hoped for.
Almost despite myself, my unspoken prayers
were answered.
I am, among all men, most richly blessed.

A CIVIL WAR SOLDIER

O God, from whom come all holy desires,
all good counsels, and all just works,
give to me, your servant, that peace
which the world cannot give,
that my heart may be set to obey in peace and
quietness; through Jesus Christ, my Lord.

ANONYMOUS

$\mathcal{K}$eep us, O God, from pettiness; let us be large in
thought, in word, in deed.
Let us be done with faultfinding
and leave off self-seeking.
May we put away all pretenses and meet each other,
face to face, without self-pity and without prejudice.
May we never be hasty in judgment
and always generous.
Let us take time for all things; make us to
grow calm, serene, gentle.
Teach us to put in action our better impulses—
straightforward and unafraid.
Grant that we may realize it is the little things of life
that create difficulties; that in the
big things of life we are as one.
Oh, Lord, let us not forget to be kind.

MARY STEWART

*I*f there be some weaker one,
God give me strength to help him on;
If a blinder soul there be,
Let me guide him nearer Thee,
Make my mortal dreams come true,
With work I fain would do;
Clothe with life the weak intent,
Let me be the thing I meant;
Let me find in Thy employ,
Peace that dearer is than joy;
Out of self to love be led,
And to heaven acclaimed;
Until all things sweet and good,
Seem my nature's habitude.

JOHN WHITTIER

I think over again my small adventures.
My fears,
Those small ones that seemed so big,
For all the vital things
I had to get and reach.
And yet there is only one great thing,
The only thing,
To live to see the great day that dawns
And the light that fills the world.

AN INUIT INDIAN PRAYER

$\mathcal{L}$et us know peace.
For as long as the moon shall rise,
For as long as the rivers shall flow,
For as long as the sun shall shine,
For as long as the grass shall grow,
Let us know peace.

AMERICAN INDIAN PRAYER FOR PEACE

FAITH

*M*ay all in this world be happy,
may they be healthy,
may they be comfortable
and never miserable.

May the rain come down in the proper time,
may the earth yield plenty of corn,
may the country be free from war,
may the Brahmans be secure.

HINDU MORNING PRAYER

In Thy name, Lord, I lay me down and
in Thy name will I rise up . . .

ISLAMIC BEDTIME PRAYER

God,

Thou art the first and before Thee there is nothing;
Thou art the last and after Thee there is nothing;
Thou art the outmost and above Thee there is nothing;
Thou art the inmost and below Thee there is nothing . . .

Waken me, O God, in the hour most pleasing to Thee
and use me in the works most pleasing to Thee,
that Thou mayest bring me ever nearer to Thyself . . .

AL-GHAZALI

$\mathcal{B}$lessed are you, Lord our God, king of the universe, who causes the bonds of sleep to fall on my eyes, and slumber on my eyelids.

May it be acceptable in your presence, O Lord my God, and God of my fathers, to cause me to lie down in peace, and to raise me up again in peace; and suffer me not to be troubled with evil dreams, or evil reflections; but grant me a calm and uninterrupted repose in your presence; and enlighten my eyes again, lest I sleep the sleep of death.

Blessed are you, O Lord, who gives light to the whole universe in your glory . . .

JEWISH BEDTIME PRAYER

$\mathscr{G}$rant us Lord, God, that while our bodies rest from the labors of the day and as our souls are released from the thoughts of this world, we may stand in Thy presence with tranquility and quietness in this evening hour.

Make us worthy to offer Thee ceaseless praise and thanksgiving without interruption.

May we acknowledge Thy loving kindness and mercy by which Thou dost rule and direct and save our souls.

Unto Thee we offer praise and thanksgiving now and unto ages of ages.

CHRISTIAN BEDTIME PRAYER

Father, we thank Thee,
For flowers that bloom about our feet,
Father, we thank Thee,
For tender grass so fresh and sweet,
Father, we thank Thee,
For the song of bird and hum of bee,
For all things fair we hear or see,
Father in heaven, we thank Thee.
For blue of stream and blue of sky,
Father, we thank Thee,
For pleasant shade of branches high,
Father, we thank Thee,
For fragrant air and cooling breeze,
For beauty of the blooming trees,
Father in heaven, we thank Thee.

For this new morning with its light,
Father, we thank Thee,
For rest and shelter of the night,
Father, we thank Thee,
For health and food, for love and friends,
For everything Thy goodness sends,
Father in heaven, we thank Thee.

RALPH WALDO EMERSON

$\mathcal{A}$lmighty God Who art the Author of Liberty and the Champion of the oppressed hear our prayer.

We the men of Special Forces, acknowledge our dependence upon Thee in the preservation of human freedom. Go with us as we seek to defend the defenseless and to free the enslaved.

May we ever remember that our nation, whose oath "in God We Trust," expects that we shall requite ourselves with honor, that we may never bring shame upon our faith, our families, or our fellow men.

Grant us wisdom from Thy mind, courage from Thine heart, and protection by Thine hand. It is for Thee that we do battle, and to Thee belongs the victor's crown. For Thine is the kingdom, and the power and glory forever, Amen!

ANONYMOUS

Our Father, which art in heaven,
Hallowed be Thy name.
Thy kingdom come,
Thy will be done in earth, as it is in heaven.
Give us this day our daily bread,
And forgive us our debts, as we forgive our debtors.
And lead us not into temptation,
But deliver us from evil:
For Thine is the Kingdom, and the power,
and the glory, forever.
Amen.

MATTHEW 6:9-13

$\mathcal{G}$od grant me
Serenity to accept the things I cannot change,
Courage to change the things I can, and
Wisdom to know the difference.

Living one day at a time;
enjoying one moment at a time;
accepting hardship
as the pathway to peace.

Taking, as He did, this sinful world
as it is, not as I would have it;
trusting that He will make all things right
if I surrender to His will;
that I may be reasonably happy in this life
and supremely happy with Him forever in the next.

THE SERENITY PRAYER

Where the mind is without fear
and the head is held high;
Where knowledge is free;
Where the world has not been broken up into
fragments by narrow domestic wars;
Where words come out from the depth of truth;
Where tireless striving stretches its arms
towards perfection;
Where the clear stream of reason has not lost its way
into the dreary desert sand of dead habit;
Where the mind is led forward by thee into
ever-widening thought and action—
Into that heaven of freedom, my Father,
let my country awake.

RABINDRANATH TAGORE

$\mathscr{C}$hrist be with me, Christ within me,
Christ behind me, Christ before me,
Christ beside me, Christ to win me,
Christ to comfort and restore me,
Christ beneath me, Christ above me,
Christ in quiet, Christ in danger,
Christ in hearts of all that love me,
Christ in mouth of friend and stranger.

ST. PATRICK'S BREASTPLATE

O gracious and holy Father,
Give us wisdom to perceive you,
intelligence to understand you,
diligence to seek you,
patience to wait for you,
eyes to see you,
a heart to meditate on you,
and a life to proclaim you,
through the power of the spirit of
Jesus Christ our Lord.

ST. BENEDICT

*L*isten to the salutation to the dawn,
Look to this day for it is life, the very life of life,
In its brief course lie all the verities and
realities of our existence.
The bliss of growth, the splendor of beauty,
For yesterday is but a dream and
tomorrow is only a vision,
But today well spent makes every yesterday
a dream of happiness
and every tomorrow a vision of hope.
Look well therefore to this day.
Such is the salutation to the dawn.

SANSKRIT SALUTATION TO THE DAWN

O God,
You are Peace.
From You comes Peace,
To You returns Peace.
Revive us with a salutation of peace,
And lead us to your abode of Peace.

ISLAMIC PRAYER OF PEACE

Now I lay me down to sleep,
I pray the Lord my soul to keep.
Four corners to my bed,
Four angels there aspread:
Two to foot and two to head,
And four to carry me when I'm dead.
If any danger come to me,
Sweet Jesus Christ deliver me.
And if I die before I wake,
I pray the Lord my soul to take.

A BEDSIDE PRAYER

$\mathcal{L}$ead me from Death to Life,
from Falsehood to Truth.
Lead me from Despair to Hope, from Fear to Trust.
Lead me from Hate to Love, from War to Peace.
Let Peace fill our Heart, our World, our Universe.

PRAYER FOR PEACE (JAIN)

May there always be work for your hands to do
May your purse always hold a coin or two
May the sun always shine upon your windowpane
May a rainbow be certain to follow each rain
May the hand of a friend always be near to you and
May God fill your heart with gladness to cheer you.

IRISH PRAYER

May the road rise up to meet you,
May the wind be always at your back,
May the sun shine warm on your face,
The rain fall softly on your fields;
And until we meet again,
May God hold you in the palm of His hand.

GAELIC PRAYER FOR ST. PATRICK'S DAY

When each day is sacred
When each hour is sacred
When each instant is sacred
Earth and you
Space and you
Bearing the sacred
Through time
You'll reach
the fields of light.

GUILLEVIC

Glorious God, give me grace to amend my life, and
to have an eye to my end without begrudging death,
which to those who die in you, good Lord,
is the gate of a wealthy life.

And give me, good Lord, a humble, lowly, quiet, peace-
able, patient, charitable, kind, tender and pitiful mind,
in all my works and all my words and all my thoughts,
to have a taste of your holy, blessed Spirit.

Give me, good Lord, a full faith, a firm hope,
and a fervent charity, a love of you incomparably
above the love of myself.

Give me, good Lord, a longing to be with you, not to
avoid the calamities of this world, nor so much to attain
the joys of heaven, as simply for love of you.

And give me, good Lord, your love and favor, which my
love of you, however great it might be, could not
deserve were it not for your great goodness.

These things, good Lord, that I pray for,
give me your grace to labor for.

THOMAS MOORE

*J*esus, our Master, meet us while we walk in the way, and long to reach the heavenly country; so that, following your light we may keep the way of righteousness, and never wander away into the darkness of this world's night, while you, who are the Way, the Truth, and the Life, are shining within us; for your own name's sake.

THE MOZARABIC PRAYER
ANCIENT SPANISH LITURGY

Lord, I believe in you.
Lord, I hope in you.

Lord, I love you.
Lord, hear me.
Lord, increase my faith.

Lord Jesus Christ,
Son of the living God,
Have mercy on me.

FATHER VICTOR HOAGLAND

*L*ord, may everything that I do start well
and finish well. Sustain me with your power.
And in your power let me drive away all falsehood,
ensuring that truth may always triumph.

PROPHET MUHAMMAD

I do not ask for fame, for a high position in
society, for a palace in which to live.
I do not ask for the company of clever and witty people.
Such ambitions mean nothing to me.
I desire only you, Lord of life.
Your love makes my heart melt like butter.
Your grace gives a taste like honey on my tongue.
Your goodness is as soft as silk upon my skin.
Your beauty makes my eyes sparkle with joy.
I want nothing but you.

MANIKKA VASAHAR

$\mathcal{G}$rant us, O God, your protection;
and in your protection, strength;
and in strength, understanding;
and in understanding, knowledge;
and in knowledge, the knowledge of justice;
and in the knowledge of justice, the love of justice;
and in that love, the love of existence;
and in the love of existence, the love of God,
God and all goodness.

WELSH PRAYER

Cultivate friendship which will
conquer all hearts.
Look upon others as thyself.
Renounce war; Forswear competition.
Give up aggression on others, as this is wrong.
Wide mother earth, our mother,
is here ready to give us all desires.
We have the Lord, our Father, compassionate to all.
Ye people of the world! Restrain yourselves.
Give, be kind.
May all people be happy and prosperous.
May all people be happy and prosperous.

JAGATGURU SHRI SANKARACHARYA

*O*pen to us, Lord, your great Door,
O Fountain of all mercy, hear our prayer and
have mercy on our souls.
Lord of the morning and ruler of all seasons,
hear our prayer and have mercy on our souls.
Shine upon me, Lord, and I shall be Light like the
day. I will sing your praise in Light while I marvel.
May the morning awaken me to the praise of your
Godhead and I will pursue the study
of your Word all the day long.
With the day may your Light shine on our thoughts
and may it drive away the shadows of error
from our souls.
The creation is full of Light, give Light also to our
hearts that they may praise you
with the day and the night.
Rise up, O children of Light, and let us give glory to
the Lord who alone can save our souls.
O Lord, as you withdraw sleep from the eyes of our body,
grant us wakefulness of mind so that we may stand
before you in awe and sing your praises worthily.

ORTHODOX PRAYER

Now I lay me down to sleep.
I pray Thee, Lord, my soul to keep.
Thy Angels guard me through the night
And keep me safe 'til morning light.

Help me to know Thy Love for me
So I a loving child may be,
With generous thoughts and happy face
And pleasant words in every place.

Teach me to always say what's true,
Be willing in each task I do.
Please help me to be good each day,
And lead me in Thy Holy way.

I pray whatever wrongs I've done
You will forgive them, every one.
Be near me when I wake again,
And bless all those I love.

A CHILD'S PRAYER

*D*irect my thoughts, words and work, wash away my sins in the immaculate Blood of the Lamb, and purge my Heart by Thy Holy Spirit. . . . Daily Frame me more and more into the likeness of Thy Son Jesus Christ.

GEORGE WASHINGTON

Softly now the light of day
Fades upon my sight away.
Free from care, from labor free,
Lord, I would commune with thee.

GEORGE W. DOANE

I pray Heaven bestow the best of blessings on this House and all that shall hereafter inhabit it. May none but honest and wise men ever rule under this roof.

JOHN ADAMS

O God, help us in our lives and in
all of our attitudes,
to work out this controlling force of love,
this controlling power that can solve
every problem that we confront in all areas.
Oh, we talk about politics;
we talk about the problems facing
our atomic civilization.
Grant that all men will come together and discover
that as we solve the crisis and solve these problems,
the international problems,
the problems of atomic energy,
the problems of nuclear energy,
and yes, even the race problem;
let us join together in a great fellowship of love
and bow down at the feet of Jesus.
Give us this strong determination.
In the name and spirit of this Christ, we pray.

MARTIN LUTHER KING JR.

$\mathcal{G}$od our strength, you are the only refuge
of all who trust you.
Fortify us with your goodness to live in
quietness of spirit,
that we may serve you all our days;
through Jesus Christ, your Son. Amen.

PSALM PRAYER

We pray to you, almighty God, in this time of conflict. You are our refuge and our strength, a very present help in time of trouble. Do not let us fail in the face of these events. Uphold us with your love and give us the strength we need. Help us in our confusion, and guide our actions. Heal the hurt, console the bereaved and afflicted, protect the innocent and helpless, and deliver any who are still in peril; for the sake of your great mercy in Jesus Christ our Lord. Amen.

OCCASIONAL SERVICES (LUTHERAN)
PRAYER IN TIME OF CONFLICT

*L*ord, since You exist, we exist.
Since You are beautiful,
We are beautiful.
Since You are good,
We are good.
By our existence we honor You.
By our beauty we glorify You.
By our goodness we love You.

EDMUND OF ABINGTON

Oh, Lord, I've never lived where churches grow,
I love creation better as it stood
That day You finished it so long ago
And looked upon Your work and called it good.
I know that others find You in the light
That's sifted down through tinted window panes,
And yet I seem to feel You near tonight
In this dim, quiet starlight on the plains.

I thank You, Lord, that I am placed so well,
That You have made my freedom so complete;
That I'm no slave of whistle, clock or bell,
Nor weak-eyed prisoner of wall and street.
Just let me live my life as I've begun
And give me work that's open to the sky;
Make me a pardner of the wind and sun,
And I won't ask a life that's soft or high.

BADGER CLARK, "A COWBOY'S PRAYER"

GLORY

The Lord our God be with us, as He was with our fathers; may He not leave us or forsake us; so that He may incline our hearts to Him, to walk in all His ways . . . that all peoples of the earth may know that the Lord is God; there is no other.

GEORGE BUSH

I worship you in every religion that teaches
your laws and praises your glory.
I worship you in every plant whose beauty
reflects your beauty.
I worship you in every event which is caused
by your goodness and kindness.
I worship you in every place where you dwell.
And I worship you in every man and woman who
seeks to follow your way of righteousness.

ZOROASTER

*P*eace I leave with you, my peace I give you:
Not as the world giveth, give I unto you.
Let not your heart be troubled,
neither let it be afraid.

JOHN 14:27

Christ, why do you allow wars and massacres on earth? By what mysterious judgment do you allow innocent people to be cruelly slaughtered?

I cannot know. I can only find assurance in the promise that your people will find peace in heaven, where no one makes war.

As gold is purified by fire, so you purify souls by these bodily tribulations, making them ready to be received above the stars in your heavenly home.

ALCUIN OF YORK

*D*earest Lord, teach me to be generous,
Teach me to serve You as I should,
To give and not to count the cost,
To fight and not to heed the wounds,
To toil and not to seek for rest,
To labour and ask not for reward,
Save that of knowing that I do Your most holy will.

ST. IGNATIUS LOYOLA

$\mathcal{G}$od is our refuge and strength,
a tested help in times of trouble.

And so we need not fear even if the world blows up,
and the mountains crumble into the sea.

Let the oceans roar and foam;
let the mountains tremble!

There is a river of joy flowing through the City of our
God—the sacred home of the God above all gods.

God himself is living in that City;
therefore it stands unmoved despite the turmoil
everywhere. He will not delay his help.

The nations rant and rave in anger—but when
God speaks, the earth melts in submission and
kingdoms totter into ruin.

The Commander of the armies of heaven
is here among us. He, the God of Jacob,
has come to rescue us.

Come, see the glorious things that our God does,
how he brings ruin upon the world,

And causes wars to end throughout the earth,
breaking and burning every weapon.

"Stand silent! Know that I am God! I will be
honored by every nation in the world!"

The Commander of the heavenly armies
is here among us! He, the God of Jacob,
has come to rescue us!

PSALM 46

I need thee every hour, most gracious Lord.
No tender voice like thine, can peace afford.
I need thee, oh, I need thee; every hour I need thee!
Oh, bless me now, my Savior; I come to thee!

ANNIE S. HAWKES

Precious Savior, dear Redeemer,
thy sweet message now impart.
May thy Spirit, pure and fervid, enter ev'ry timid heart;
Carry there the swift conviction, turning back the sinful tide.
Precious Savior, dear Redeemer, may each soul in thee abide.

Precious Savior, dear Redeemer,
we are weak but thou art strong;
In thy infinite compassion, stay the tide of sin and wrong.
Keep thy loving arms around us; keep us in the narrow way.
Precious Savior, dear Redeemer, let us never from thee stray.

Precious Savior, dear Redeemer,
thou wilt bind the broken heart.
Let not sorrow overwhelm us; dry the bitter tears that start.
Curb the winds and calm the billows;
bid the angry tempest cease.
Precious Savior, dear Redeemer, grant us everlasting peace.

H. R. PALMER

Jesus, Savior, pilot me over life's tempestuous sea;
Unknown waves before me roll,
hiding rock and treach'rous shoal.
Chart and compass came from thee:
Jesus, Savior, pilot me.

As a mother stills her child,
thou canst hush the ocean wild;
Boist'rous waves obey thy will when thou say'st to them,
"Be still!"
Wondrous Sov'reign of the sea, Jesus, Savior, pilot me.

When at last I near the shore,
and the fearful breakers roar
'Twixt me and the peaceful rest,
then, while leaning on thy breast,
May I hear thee say to me, "Fear not: I will pilot thee."

EDWARD HOPPER

*F*ather in Heaven, in thy love abounding,
Hear these thy children thru the world resounding, loud
in thy praises.
Thanks for peace abiding, ever abiding.

Filled be our hearts with peace beyond comparing, peace
in thy world,
And joy to hearts despairing.
Firm is our trust in thee for peace enduring,
Ever enduring.

God of our fathers, strengthen ev'ry nation.
In thy great peace, where only is salvation.
So may the world its future spread before thee,
thus to adore thee.

ANGUS S. HIBBARD

*S*weet hour of prayer! Sweet hour of prayer!
That calls me from a world of care.
And bids me at my Father's throne
make all my wants and wishes known.
In seasons of distress and grief,
my soul has often found relief.
And oft escaped the tempter's snare
By thy return, sweet hour of prayer!

Sweet hour of prayer! Sweet hour of prayer!
Thy wings shall my petition bear
To him whose truth and faithfulness
engage the waiting soul to bless.
And since he bids me seek his face,
believe his word, and trust his grace,
I'll cast on him my ev'ry care, and wait for thee,
sweet hour of prayer!

WILLIAM W. WALFORD

God be with you till we meet again;
By his counsels guide, uphold you;
With his sheep securely fold you.
God be with you till we meet again.

God be with you till we meet again;
When life's perils thick confound you,
Put his arms unfailing round you.
God be with you till we meet again.

God be with you till we meet again;
Keep love's banner floating o'er you;
Smite death's threatening wave before you.
God be with you till we meet again.
Till we meet, till we meet,
Till we meet, till we meet, at Jesus' feet.
God be with you till we meet again.

JEREMIAH E. RANKIN

$\mathcal{L}$ord, we ask thee ere we part,
Bless the teachings of this day.
Plant them deep in ev'ry heart,
That with us they'll ever stay.

In the innocence of youth,
We would all thy laws fulfill.
Lead us in the way of truth.
Give us strength to do thy will.

Father, merciful and kind,
While we labor for the right,
May we in thy service find.
Sweetest pleasure, pure delight.

All of our follies, Lord, forgive.
Keep us from temptations free.
Help us evermore to live
Lives of holiness to thee.

GEORGE MANWARING

*N*ow the day is over;
Night is drawing nigh;
Shadows of the evening
Steal across the sky.

Jesus, give the weary
Calm and sweet repose;
With thy tend'rest blessing
May our eyelids close.

SABINE BARING-GOULD

*W*here there is charity and wisdom,
there is neither fear nor ignorance.
Where there is patience and humility,
there is neither anger nor vexation.
Where there is poverty and joy,
there is neither greed nor avarice.
Where there is peace and meditation,
there is neither anxiety nor doubt.

ST. FRANCIS OF ASSISI

As watchmen wait for the morning,
so do our souls long for you, O Christ.
Come with the dawning of the day,
and make yourself known to us in the breaking of
bread; for you are our God for ever and ever.

THE MOZARABIC MORNING PRAYER
ANCIENT SPANISH LITURGY

Abide with me; 'tis eventide.
The day is past and gone;
The shadows of the evening fall;
The night is coming on.
Within my heart a welcome guest,
within my home abide.
O Savior, stay this night with me;
Behold 'tis eventide.
O Savior, stay this night with me;
Behold 'tis eventide.

LOWRIE M. HOFFORD

$\mathcal{O}$h, thank the Lord for grace and gifts
Renewed in latter days, for truth and light to
Guide us right in wisdom's pleasant ways.

Oh, may we sleep and wake in joy,
While life with us remains,
And then go home beyond the tomb,
Where peace forever reigns.

WILLIAM W. PHELPS

O my Father, thou that dwellest
In the high and glorious place,
When shall I regain thy presence
And again behold thy face?
In thy holy habitation,
Did my spirit once reside?
In my first primeval childhood,
Was I nurtured near thy side?

ELIZA R. SNOW

*G*reat God, to thee my evening song
   With humble gratitude I raise;
Oh, let thy mercy tune my tongue
And fill my heart with lively praise.

ANNE STEELE

*L*ord, dismiss us with thy blessing;
Fill our hearts with joy and peace.
Let us each, thy love possessing,
Triumph in redeeming grace.
Oh, refresh us, oh, refresh us,
Trav'ling through this wilderness.
Oh, refresh us, oh, refresh us,
Trav'ling through this wilderness.

JOHN FAWCETT

$\mathcal{G}$rant we all may seek and find
Thee, our gracious God, and kind.
Heal the sick, the captive free.
Let us all rejoice in thee.

WILLIAM HAMMOND

O thou by whom we come to God,
The Life, the Truth, the Way!
The path of prayer thyself hast trod;
Lord, teach us how to pray.

JAMES MONTGOMERY

LIFE

*M*ore purity give me,
More strength to o'ercome,
More freedom from earth stains,
More longing for home.
More fit for the kingdom,
More used would I be,
More blessed and holy—
More, Savior, like thee.

PHILIP PAUL BLISS

$\mathcal{L}$ord, the psalmist cannot find enough words
to express trust in You.
Stir in our hearts today
Your holy spirit.
Touch the soul of this Nation that we may see your
saving work in our work,
Your strength behind our weakness,
Your purpose in our efforts at laws of justice,
Your peace drawing all of us and the whole world
to lasting freedom.

DANIEL P. COUGHLIN

All praise is for God, the Lord of the worlds.
The compassionate, the merciful.
Master of the day of judgment.
O God, You alone we worship and You alone
we call on for help.
O God, guide us to the straight way.

IMAM BASSAM A. ESTWANI

$\mathcal{G}$od bless all those that I love;
God bless all those that love me.
God bless all those that love those that I love
And all those that love those that love me.

FROM AN OLD ENGLAND SAMPLER

Day by day, O Lord, three things I pray:
To see thee more clearly, love thee more dearly,
Follow thee more clearly,
Day by day.

ST. RICHARD OF CHICHESTER

*B*eloved Lord, Almighty God,
Through the Rays of the Sun,
Through the Waves of the Air,
Through the All Pervading Life in Space;
Purify and Revivify Us
And we pray, heal our bodies, hearts, and souls.

**NAYAZ, THE HEALING PRAYER,
PIR-O-MURSHID INAYAT KHAN**

PEACE

$\mathcal{G}$ive peace in our time, O Lord.

$\mathcal{D}$eep peace of the running wave to you.
Deep peace of the flowing air to you.
Deep peace of the quiet earth to you.
Deep peace of the shining stars to you.
Deep peace of the infinite peace to you.

ANCIENT GAELIC RUNES

$\mathcal{G}$od grant that the light of unity
May envelop the whole earth,
And that the seal, "Thy Kingdom is God's,"
May be stamped upon the brow of all its peoples.

BAHA'I PRAYER

$\mathcal{L}$ord, put courage in my heart, and take away all
that may hinder me serving you.
Free my tongue to proclaim your goodness,
that all may understand me.
Give me friends to advise and help me,
that by working together our efforts
may bear abundant fruit.
And, above all, let me constantly remember that my
actions are unless they are guided by your hand.

PROPHET MUHAMMAD

𝒪 Lord, convert the world—and begin with me.

CHINESE STUDENT

*D*earest children, God is near you,
  Watching o'er you day and night,
And delights to own and bless you,
  If you strive to do what's right.
        He will bless you,
        He will bless you,
    If you put your trust in him.

CHARLES L. WALKER

$\mathcal{L}$ighten our darkness, we beseech thee, O Lord;
And by thy great mercy defend us from all perils
and dangers of this night.

PRAYER BOOK

*D*ear God,

Deliver me to my passion.

Deliver me to my brilliance.

Deliver me to my intelligence.

Deliver me to my depth.

Deliver me to my nobility.

Deliver me to my health.

Deliver me to my wealth.

Deliver me to my beauty.

Deliver me to my power to heal.

Deliver me to you.

ELIZABETH

GIBBS SMITH, PUBLISHER